Samantha and the Bully

Written and illustrated by

Charles Ray

North Potomac, MD

Copyright © 2014 Charles Ray

All rights reserved

ISBN: 0692315543
ISBN-13: 978-0692315545

One sunny day Samantha and her friends went to the park near the school to play. It was a perfect day.

Samantha and Henry were building a sand castle.

Samantha's other friends were having fun doing other things.

Yun-hi and Joe were bouncing up and down on the see-saw.

Wilson liked to see how high he could swing.

Henry's brother, Charles, enjoyed sitting under a tree reading his favorite books.

Samantha and her friends were having so much fun. It was truly a perfect day.

But, Garfield the neighborhood bully didn't like to see others having so much fun. He decided that he would ruin their perfect day.

First, he snatched the books that Charles was reading, and ran away with them.

"Hey," Charles cried. "Give me back my books!"

That was not enough for Garfield. So, he grabbed the swing, causing Wilson to fall on his face. "Oof, that hurts," Wilson said.

Garfield smiled. He was really ruining their perfect day. But, he wasn't finished yet. He saw the sand castle that Samantha and Henry were building, and he knew just what to do.

He walked over and kicked the sand castle until it was just a pile of sand.

"Oh no," Wilson cried. "You've ruined our sand castle."

Garfield laughed. "So what," he said. "What are you going to do about it?"

That made Samantha angry. She did not like to see her friends so sad. She stood and faced Garfield.

"You are a mean bully," she said. "You have ruined our perfect day."

"Hah," Garfield said. "What will you do about it?"

Samantha wanted to punch him on the nose. But, her parents always told her that fighting was not the way to solve problems. Samantha was a smart girl, though, and she knew just what to do.

"I'm going to tell the teacher what you did," she said. "And then, I'm going to tell my mom and dad. They will tell your mom and dad, and you'll be in big trouble."

Garfield looked worried. If Samantha told the teacher, he would have to stay after class, and couldn't come to the park. If her mom and dad told his mom and dad, he would not be able to go out and play, or watch TV.

"Uh, please don't tell on me," he said.

"If you say you're sorry, I won't tell," Samantha said.

A red-faced Garfield apologized to everyone, and then with his shoulders slumped, walked away.

All of Samantha's friends crowded around her, smiling and cheering.

"Hooray, Samantha!" they shouted. "You're our hero. You made the bully go away."

"My dad says that bullies are all cowards," she said. "And, if you stand up to them, they'll run away."

Samantha knew just what to do about a bully, because she listened to her mom and dad.

Now, she and her friends could have fun.

It was once again a perfect day.

Do you know what to do if a bully bothers you?